D1765133

FACT CAT

WEATHER

Izzi Howell

WITHDRAWN

3 8002 02376 281 0

FACT CAT

Get your paws on this fantastic new mega-series from Wayland!

Join our Fact Cat on a journey of fun learning about every subject under the sun!

Published in Great Britain in 2018 by Wayland
Copyright © Wayland 2016

All rights reserved
ISBN: 978 1 5263 0602 9
Dewey Number:
10 9 8 7 6 5 4 3 2 1

FSC
MIX
Paper from responsible sources
FSC® C104740

Wayland
An imprint of Hachette Children's Group
Part of Hodder & Stoughton
Carmelite House
50 Victoria Embankment
London EC4Y 0DZ

An Hachette UK Company
www.hachette.co.uk
www.hachettechildrens.co.uk

A catalogue for this title is available from
the British Library
Printed and bound in China

Produced for Wayland by
White-Thomson
www.wtpub.co.uk

Editor: Izzi Howell
Design: Clare Nicholas
Fact Cat illustrations: Shu
Other illustrations: Stefan
Consultant: Karina Philip

Picture and illustration credits:
iStock: Byrdyak 4br, stanley45 5t, Jonathan Woodcock 5b, AlinaMD 6–7t, aleksask 7b, sripfoto 9, 4FR 11, Ron Thomas 13, David Parsons 15, LuVo 19, AlesVeluscek 21; Shutterstock: Anna Omelchenko cover, Fedor Selivanov title page and 16, Mihai Simonia 4tl, liseykina 4tr, Pakhnyushchy 4 bl, Triff 6b, Suzanne Tucker 8t, C_Eng-Wong Photography 8b, Stephane Bidouze 10t and 10b, Kamira 12, kavram 14, Kichigin 17, Phill Beale 18, Dustie 20l, Minerva Studio 20r.

Every effort has been made to clear copyright. Should there be any inadvertent omission, please apply to the publisher for rectification.

The author, Izzi Howell, is a writer and editor specialising in children's educational publishing.

The consultant, Karina Philip, is a teacher and a primary literacy consultant with an MA in creative writing.

FACT CAT FACT

There is a question for you to answer on each spread in this book. You can check your answers on page 24.

Coventry City Council

FML

3 8002 02376 281 0

Askews & Holts	Mar-2018
J551.6 JUNIOR NON-FI	£7.99

CONTENTS

WHAT IS WEATHER?

Weather is the name that we give to **temperature** and outdoor **conditions**, such as rain and wind. The weather is always changing and is usually different every day.

Lightning, sunshine, clouds and snow are all types of weather.

Weather changes throughout the year depending on what season it is. There are four season in a year - spring, summer, autumn and winter. Each season has different types of weather but they often overlap.

It often rains in spring. Plants grow well in the wet weather. Which season usually has hot weather and sunshine?

FACT CAT FACT

The weather is cold all year round at the North and South Poles.

North Pole

South Pole

SUNSHINE

Sunshine comes from the Sun. The Sun is the closest star to Earth. The Sun is so hot that its light and heat can be seen and felt on Earth.

FACT CAT FACT

It takes eight minutes for light to travel from the Sun to Earth.

This photograph of the Sun was taken with a **telescope**. Why must you never look straight at the Sun?

The sun shines every day in most places on Earth. In places close to the **equator**, the sunshine is stronger and hotter because these areas are nearer to the Sun.

Sunny days are warm and bright.

When sunlight shines through the rain, a rainbow is made.

CLOUDS

Clouds are made of **water vapour**. The water in seas and rivers turns into water vapour when it is heated by the Sun. This water vapour rises into the sky, where it forms clouds.

There are many types of cloud. Cumulus (kyoom-yew-luss) clouds are puffy.

Cirrus (sih-rus) clouds look like long strings in the sky.

Some clouds form close to the ground. Other clouds (such as cirrus clouds) form high in the sky. Cirrus clouds are found at heights of 5,000 metres above the ground.

Clouds that are close to the ground are called mist or fog. What is the difference between mist and fog?

FACT CAT FACT

Clouds look white when they **reflect** light from the Sun.

RAIN

When water vapour in clouds cools down, it turns into drops of water. Sometimes these drops of water fall from clouds as rain.

These girls are using an umbrella to keep them dry from the rain.

FACT CAT FACT

Raindrops are usually less than 5 millimetres wide. In this photo, you can see the size of the raindrops compared to some leaves and berries.

In some parts of the world, it rains from time to time in every season. In other places, it rains heavily during the rainy season.

It rains almost every day in tropical rainforests. Why does it take a long time for rain to reach the ground in rainforests?

WIND

Although we can't see it, the air around us is always moving. Moving air is called wind.

The branches of these palm trees are moving in the wind.

We can make **electricity** from wind. When the wind makes the **sails** on these wind turbines move round, it makes electricity. We use electricity to **power** lights and machines.

Wind turbines are noisy. They are usually built far from towns and cities.

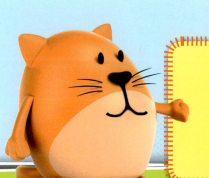

FACT CAT FACT

Strong wind is sometimes called 'a gale'. What kind of wind is 'a breeze'?

STORMS

In a storm, it rains heavily and there are strong, fast-moving winds. These winds can be dangerous, as they can knock over trees and blow things around.

Storm clouds are dark grey and full of rain.

In thunderstorms, you can see flashes of lightning and hear thunder. Lightning happens when there is electricity in clouds.

We always see lightning before we hear thunder. Why is this?

FACT CAT FACT

Lightning is five times hotter than the **surface** of the Sun!

SNOW

When the temperature in the sky is cold, water **freezes** inside clouds. If it is also cold on the ground, frozen water falls from the clouds as snow.

In some places, a thick layer of snow covers the ground in winter. What is another name for a snow storm?

Snowflakes are made of **ice crystals** (lots of frozen drops of water joined together). Snowflakes are very small. They can only be seen clearly through a **microscope**.

FACT CAT FACT

There are around two hundred ice crystals in every snowflake!

This is what snowflakes look like under a microscope.

ICE

When the temperature drops below zero degrees Celsius, water freezes into ice. Ice is hard, smooth and very cold.

The water dripping off the roof of this house has frozen into **icicles**.

FACT CAT FACT

If you place a container of hot water and a container of cold water in a freezer at the same time, the hot water will turn into ice faster than the cold water!

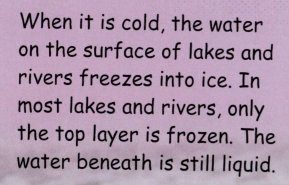

When it is cold, the water on the surface of lakes and rivers freezes into ice. In most lakes and rivers, only the top layer is frozen. The water beneath is still liquid.

It can be very dangerous to walk or skate on thin ice. Always check with an adult first.

When lakes and rivers freeze in cold weather, birds such as ducks stand on the ice. Can seas and oceans freeze?

DANGEROUS WEATHER

Tornadoes happen when strong winds **spin** inside a storm cloud. These spinning winds make a **column** that moves across the ground.

Tornadoes can travel at up to 500 kilometres per hour. In which country do over a thousand tornadoes happen every year?

Tornadoes are very dangerous. They often destroy trees and houses.

Frozen raindrops, known as hailstones, often fall from clouds in cold weather. Most hailstones are small and melt soon after they reach the ground.

Large hailstones are dangerous. They can break windows.

FACT CAT FACT

The largest hailstone **on record** was found in South Dakota, USA. It weighed almost 1 kilogram and it was as big as a football!

Try to answer the questions below. Look back through the book to help you. Check your answers on page 24.

1 The Sun is a planet. True or not true?

a) true

b) not true

2 Clouds are made of water vapour. True or not true?

a) true

b) not true

3 In which habitat does it rain nearly everyday?

a) desert

b) rainforest

c) seashore

4 We hear thunder before we see lightning. True or not true?

a) true

b) not true

5 At which temperature does water freeze?

a) 10 degrees Celsius

b) 2 degrees Celsius

c) 0 degrees Celsius

6 What is a tornado?

a) a spinning column of wind

b) a large piece of ice

c) a storm with thunder and lightning

GLOSSARY

column something with a tall, narrow shape

conditions the temperature and weather in an area

crystal a transparent substance that has become solid

destroy to damage something so badly that it doesn't exist anymore

electricity energy that produces light and heat and can be used to power machines

equator an imaginary line around the middle of the Earth

freeze to turn hard and solid because of the cold

ice frozen water

icicle a long thin piece of ice that hangs from something

microscope a machine that makes small objects look bigger

on record describes something that has been officially measured and written down

power to give electricity to a machine to make it work

reflect to send light or sound back in the direction that it came from

sail a part of a windmill that moves in the wind

spin to turn around quickly

surface the top part of something

telescope a machine that makes far-away objects appear closer

temperature how hot or cold something is

water vapour many small drops of water in the air

INDEX

ANSWERS

Pages 4–21

Page 5: Summer

Page 6: Because it can damage your eyes.

Page 9: It is harder to see through fog than through mist because it's thicker.

Page 11: Because the leaves of trees and plants stop the rain from falling straight to the ground.

Page 13: Light, gentle wind

Page 15: Because light travels faster than sound.

Page 16: A blizzard

Page 19: Yes, seas and oceans can freeze.

Page 20: The USA (United States of America)

Quiz answers

1   not true – it is a star.

2   true

3   b - rainforest

4   not true – we see lightning before we hear thunder.

5   c – 0 degrees Celsius

6   a - a spinning column of wind